ALL ABOUT...

EXTRAORDINARY EGYPTIANS

I0233951

P S Quick

Andrews UK Limited

Copyright © 2012 P S Quick

The right of P S Quick to be identified as author of this book has been asserted in accordance with section 77 and 78 of the Copyrights Designs and Patents Act 1988.

All rights reserved

No part of this publication may be reproduced, stored in a retrieval system, or transmitted in any form or by any means, without the prior permission in writing of the publisher, nor be otherwise circulated in any form of binding or cover other than that in which it is published and without a similar condition including this condition being imposed on the subsequent publisher.

First published worldwide by
Andrews UK Limited
The Hat Factory
Bute Street
Luton
LU1 2EY

www.andrewsuk.com

Contents

EXTRAORDINARY
EGYPTIANS

Ancient Egypt is United

The civilization of Ancient Egypt lasted over 3000 years and was one of the most powerful in the history of the world. It covers the period from 3150 BC to 30 BC although there is evidence to suggest that farmers lived along the banks of the Nile 2000 years before this.

Egypt had been divided into two kingdoms before this time. Lower Egypt was called the kingdom of the Red Crown while Upper Egypt was known as the kingdom of the White Crown.

Many monuments and tombs still exist today, giving us evidence of this fascinating time in history.

When the pharaoh of the Red Crown conquered the south, Egypt became united and our story begins.

Everyday life

Most people lived in small houses built using mud bricks. Ancient Egyptians made the bricks by mixing soil from the River Nile with straw and shaping them by using wooden moulds. Then they were dried in the sun. The outsides were painted white to lessen the heat reaching inside. This was a cheap material for building but was not durable and long lasting.

The houses had flat roofs so people could sleep outside in the summer when it was too hot to be inside. The windows were also small, narrow and high up to keep out the sun. Houses were grouped together in small villages.

The many paintings and sculptures that have been left behind are evidence of what the people wore. Egypt is a hot country so most people wore lightweight linen clothes to keep them cool. The linen came from the flax they grew and was woven into cloth. Men wore a kind of white kilt and the women simple straight dresses but slaves and servants often wore patterned clothes.

Both men and women wore make up, mainly eye shadow of blue and green with black eyeliner. Women painted their fingernails and put red powder on their lips. Many combs, mirrors and even razors have been found proving that even the poorer people like farmers liked to groom themselves.

They also wore jewellery such as necklaces, rings and bracelets as well as good luck charms known as amulets. The rich would wear jewellery made from silver and gold but the poor would only wear copper.

The main food for the poor was bread, made from wheat, but this was so coarse it wore their teeth away. They also ate vegetables. The favourite drink was beer which was made from barley. Food was served in dishes made from clay and baked in clay ovens. They also ate fruit, vegetables and occasionally meat such as goat or lamb. Food was dried in the sun to preserve it. Honey was used to sweeten food.

Only children from the higher classes in Egypt went to school. Others would help parents with their work when old enough. Beautiful toys were made from ivory, marble, ceramics and stone. They played board games but also lots of physical games as we do today. Balls were made from leather, stuffed with things such as straw or reeds, and tied with string.

Young children played with dolls, spinning tops, skittles, toy animals and mechanical toys such as crocodiles. Not everyone could afford expensive toys so many children had toys made from clay.

Families kept pets such as dogs, monkeys, baboons and birds. Nearly every family had a cat but cats were sacred and not pets. Egyptians kept them because they believed them to have magic powers which would protect them from danger. They were also able to kill the many rats and mice which caused disease. When a cat died the whole family would shave their eyebrows as a mark of respect.

The River Nile

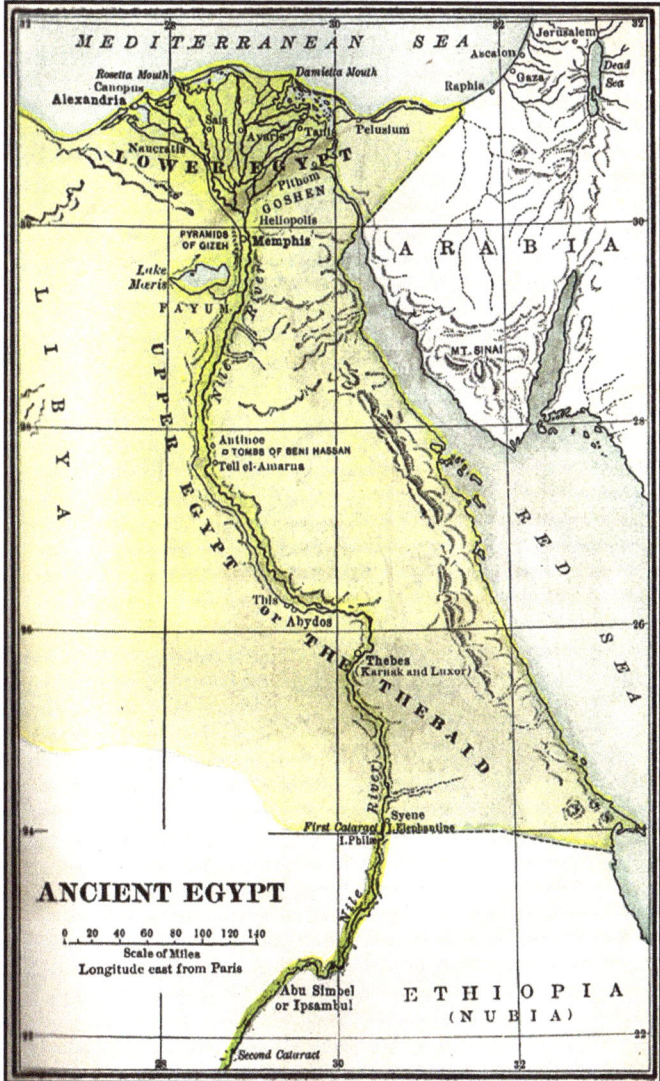

ANCIENT EGYPT

When you look at this map of Ancient Egypt you will see the River Nile flowing northwards through the middle of the country into the Mediterranean Sea. The river formed a delta where the river split into channels as it flowed between the silt. The length of the Nile River is approximately 6650 kilometres (4132 miles). It is believed to be the longest river in the world.

Egypt was known as 'The Gift of the Nile' because Egyptians relied upon the resources that this great river offered. It was their main way of transporting goods and people as well as the source of water for irrigation.

Most of Egypt was desert, where it was too hot and dry to grow crops, so the ancient civilisation lived along the banks of the River Nile. It was the source of much of the country's wealth and so many important towns and cities grew up along its banks.

The Nile itself also provided food for the Egyptians. They were able to catch its fish using spears and nets as well as the birds that lived on and besides the Nile.

Every year the melting mountain snows of spring and the heavy summer rainfall caused the River Nile to become a torrent that overflowed its banks.

Today the Nile no longer overflows as the Egyptians have built a huge dam in Aswan which holds back the water in Lake Nasser. It was completed in 1970.

About 95% of Egypt's population still live along the banks of the Nile today.

In ancient times when the River Nile flooded each year it deposited a layer of rich black silt over the land. This silt made the land very fertile so it was very good for growing food.

This land, next to the Nile, was called the Black Land, named after the dark, black silt. The Egyptians called their land Kemet, which means Black Land.

The land further from the Nile was desert and known as Deshret, meaning the Red Land as nothing would grow there. The deserts also formed a barrier between neighbouring countries and protected Egypt from invasion.

Farming

Everyone depended upon the early farmers to provide food for the Egyptians. When there was a large flood there would be a good harvest, whereas in a bad year people would starve.

When the flood waters went down the farmers would plant their crops. These had to be harvested before the next flood.

Two of the most important crops were wheat and barley, with which they made bread, porridge and beer. Another was flax, from which they made linen for clothes. The first crops that were planted each year were the grain crops. Cattle were used to help tramp the seeds into the ground.

Once the grain had been harvested they planted vegetables such as onions, leeks, beans and cabbages. Only rich people ate meat every day.

The farmers also planted fruit trees such as pomegranates and vines along the paths to give shade for the plants as well as fruit to eat.

Egyptian farmers divided their year into three seasons.

The flooding Season, known as **Akhet**, was between June and September.

Because all the fields were flooded during this time no farming could be done so they spent this time mending their tools and looking after their animals.

Some farmers would work for the pharaoh during this time, building pyramids or temples.

The Growing Season, known as **Peret**, lasted from October to February. In October, once the flood waters had receded, leaving behind the dark, rich soil, the land was ploughed and seeded.

The third season was the Harvesting Season, known as **Shemu**. During this time the crops had to be harvested before the Nile flooded again.

The Ancient Egyptians used simple tools such as hoes, rakes, sickles, scoops and ploughs. These were usually made from wood or stone but sometimes from copper. Wall paintings and buried tools show us what these were like.

Some ploughs were pushed by hand while others were pulled by Oxen.

The fertile land needed a lot of water to keep it from drying out. The Ancient Egyptians used bricks made of mud to build reservoirs. They also dug out canals which filled up the reservoirs during the floods and could be used to irrigate the crops once the floods had gone down.

To lift the water from the Nile or canals onto the land a Shaduf was used. This was a long pole with a basin or basket made of skin on one end and a weight on the other.

The reeds, called Papyrus, which grew alongside the Nile were also used. Not only did the Egyptians use these to make paper they also used them to make boats.

Using these boats on the Nile was the quickest way to travel from place to place.

The ancient Egyptians did not use money to buy things as we do today. Instead they used a barter system in which they did jobs for each other or paid using animals or crops such as wheat and barley. If someone had more than they needed of one crop they would try to exchange it for something else that they needed.

Government

The pharaoh was the supreme ruler of the government as well as of religion. People regarded him not only as a king but also a God.

However, he could not rule a whole country by himself so he had lots of helpers. Egyptian society was ruled by a hierarchy. Imagine a pyramid with the pharaoh at the top and the less important people at the bottom.

The Pharaoh was responsible for making laws and making sure Egypt was not attacked by its enemies.

The Vizier was the pharaoh's most important adviser and was sometimes also the High Priest. He was responsible for ensuring there was enough food, settling quarrels and protecting the pharaoh's household.

Priests and Nobles were responsible for making local laws and keeping order. The priests were also responsible for keeping the Gods happy.

Scribes were the only people, along with priests, who could read and write. They were responsible for such things as keeping records about how much food was produced or how many soldiers were in the army.

Soldiers were employed to protect the country. They were paid with land or by keeping things that they captured from their enemies.

Skilled Craftsmen were people such as jewellery makers, weavers, painters, tailors, carpenters and potters.

Slaves, labourers and peasants were at the bottom of the pyramid as they were not skilled. The pharaoh and his nobles gave the farmers a place to live, as well as food and clothes, in return for their labour.

The pharaoh was the king or queen of Egypt but had much more power than our monarchs. The pharaoh was the most important person in the kingdom, head of the government and the most important High Priest.

The word pharaoh means 'Great House' and this really refers to the kingdom over which he ruled. pharaohs wore a crown decorated with a cobra, representing the cobra goddess. It was said to protect them from their enemies by spitting flames.

The time for which a family ruled as pharaohs was known as a dynasty and there were thought to be 31 dynasties during Ancient Egyptian times. There were many great pharaohs who ruled during this time.

People thought pharaohs to be half man and half God. They believed that once a pharaoh had died they would not have the wonderful gifts of the sun and the River Nile if he did not make a safe journey to the afterlife.

The first pharaohs were buried, with the possessions they believed they needed, in the Egyptian sand. This meant that wild animals could find their bodies easily and destroy them, so the Ancient Egyptians built huge mud pits around the graves.

In time the Egyptians learnt how to mummify and preserve bodies and buried them in burial chambers called pyramids. However, grave robbers would steal a pharaoh's possessions, so they often put curses onto the pyramid to protect the contents.

Only the pharaohs were mummified (although some cats were also mummified) because Egyptian people believed they were the only ones who could live in the afterlife and that everyone else would go to the underworld.

Menes was the first pharaoh of Egypt. He was the person who united the north and south kingdoms of Egypt and founded the city of Memphis as its capital where the two lands met.

Ramesses II was one of the longest ruling pharaohs, ruling for 67 years. It is said he lived until he was over 80, which is an amazing age for these times as most Egyptians only lived until they were about 40. Ramesses was a great warrior and also known as a builder. He had at least twelve wives and 100 children. He is also the pharaoh who had the most monuments built to himself.

RAMSES II

Although many pharaohs were men there were some women pharaohs too. Cleopatra and Nefertiti were both women.

Nefertiti was really the great royal wife of the pharaoh Akhenaten but some people believe she ruled for a short time after her husband's death. She is always remembered for her great beauty but no-one knows how she died.

Nefertiti and her husband Akhenaten only worshipped one god. This was the sun god known as Aten (another form of Ra). They closed many of the Egyptian temples where other gods were worshipped. Akhenaten was the father of the famous pharaoh Tutankhamun.

Tutankhamun became pharaoh at the age of 9 but died at the age of 18. Many people think that he was murdered.

The reason that Tutankhamun is so famous is that his tomb, which contained many fantastic treasures, was discovered in 1922. He was buried in a tomb in the Valley of the Kings, on the west bank of the River Nile, near Luxor.

Hatshepsut was a woman who originally ruled in place of her son but she became known as one of the greatest women pharaohs. She dressed like the male pharaoh, wearing a crown and ceremonial beard.

Cleopatra VII became pharaoh at the age of 17 but died at 39. She was considered to be the last pharaoh of Egypt. She ruled at a difficult time. Not only did her brother want to be on the throne but the Romans were invading and destroying many cities.

She managed to stay in power by becoming very good friends with two leaders of the Roman army called Julius Caesar and Mark Anthony. Mark Anthony's wife, back home in Rome, was very angry about this and sent her brother, Octavian, to Egypt to kill Anthony and Cleopatra.

Octavian was successful. When Anthony was badly wounded he asked to be taken to Cleopatra and died in her arms. Cleopatra was captured and decided to kill herself with a poisonous snake called an asp.

This was the end of the era we know as the Ancient Egyptians as Egypt then became a province of Rome.

Mummification

When a person died, the Ancient Egyptians believed they had to make a journey through the Underworld before going to the Afterlife. The Afterlife was meant to be a perfect version of ancient Egypt. For this reason they wanted to preserve a body for as long as possible. They found a way to embalm bodies called Mummification.

Making a mummy was a complicated and gory job so if you are squeamish skip this next bit!

Before embalming began the body was washed in the River Nile as a sign of rebirth and to purify it.

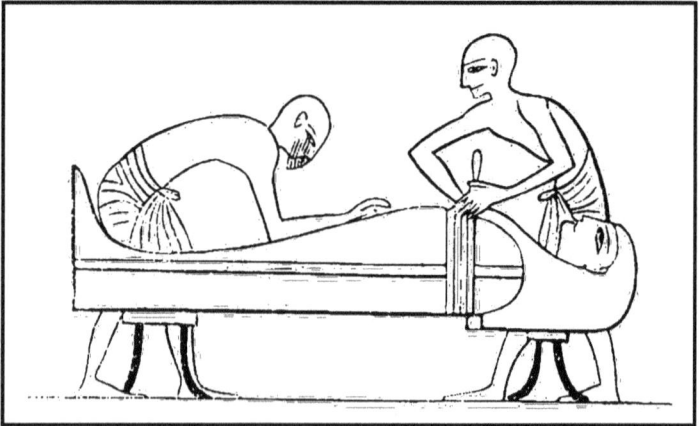

Once this was done they used a hook to remove the brain and threw it away because they thought it was worthless.

They took out the other main organs from the body and put these into special jars called 'Canopic Jars'. Each organ was put inside a different jar, and sealed with a top representing an animal or human head.

The heart was kept in the body because they believed it was the centre of intelligence and would be needed in the Afterlife. A ceremony was performed in the Afterlife, known as 'The Weighing of the Heart' to determine whether or not the person had led a good life.

After this the body was filled with a mixture of perfume and a salt called Natron before being left for 40 days to dry out.

Once the body was dry it was then stuffed with spices, sawdust, leaves and linen to help it keep its shape. The body was then sewn up and rubbed with oils to prevent it from wrinkling.

Next the body was wrapped in layers of linen bandages. When the body had been treated in this way it was called a 'Mummy'. An amulet (a good luck charm) was placed with the mummy for luck. A Death Mask was then fitted over the face.

When the time for burial arrived the mummy was wrapped in a sheet called a shroud then placed in a special box, shaped like their body, called a sarcophagus. This was then decorated with the person's portrait so that the dead person's spirit would recognise their face in the Afterlife.

After a funeral service had been held by the High Priest in the temple, the pharaoh's body was taken to the tomb. The pharaoh was buried with all his possessions so that he would have all he needed in the next life.

MUMMY CASE

The Pyramids

The pyramids, some of the most impressive structures built in ancient times, were the stone tombs and monuments of the pharaohs. The first ones were built around 4500 years ago. It is amazing that many are still standing and we can still explore them. The ruins of 35 pyramids still stand along the banks of the Nile, preserved by the hot, dry climate. The base was always a perfect square.

Because the pharaohs were buried with so many of their possessions, and have remained standing for thousands of years, their hidden secrets have given us evidence and an understanding of what life and death was like for the Ancient Egyptians.

Although some people believed the pyramids had been built by slaves they were actually built by the farmers who normally worked in the fields.

Once the Nile had flooded, and no farming could take place, these workers were free to help build the pyramids. These people believed that by helping a pharaoh reach the Afterlife they would be ensuring their own immortality, although of course ordinary people were not embalmed and buried in stone tombs.

Although it was originally thought that the huge stones, needed to build the pyramids were moved on rollers, evidence now suggests that they were pulled on sledges using ramps, before being hoisted into position. This was made easier by covering the ground with water to make the sledges move more easily.

There were different kinds of pyramids. Some of the earlier ones had larger ledges which looked like giant steps. These are known as 'Step Pyramids'. It is thought that they were built as stairways so the pharaoh could climb them to reach the sun god.

The earliest known pyramid was built about 4700 years ago at Saqqara. It is known as the stepped pyramid of Djoser, sometimes called Zozer; although the pharaoh's name was Netjerykhet, meaning 'body of the gods'.

The later pyramids have sides that are flatter and slope. They are said to represent the mound from which the Earth was created. The sun god was believed to have stood on the top and created the other gods and goddesses.

One fascinating pyramid is the 'Bent Pyramid', which can be found at Giza and was built for Pharaoh Sneferu. This pyramid, with straight sides, starts with sides sloping at a steep angle and then changes to a less steep angle.

It is the thought that a mistake was made with the angle when it was first being built. If the builders had continued to build at this angle it would have been much too high and would have required an excessive amount of labour and materials to build it.

Most pyramids were built in the desert on the western side of the River Nile. The stones were bought in boats along the Nile and the dry desert heat was perfect for preserving their contents.

The largest pyramid of all is the Giant Pyramid of Giza, built for the pharaoh Khufu. It is 139 metres tall and points directly north. Its base covers 13 acres and 2 million limestone blocks were needed to build it.

This pyramid took over 20 years to build and is recognised as one of the Seven Wonders of the World.

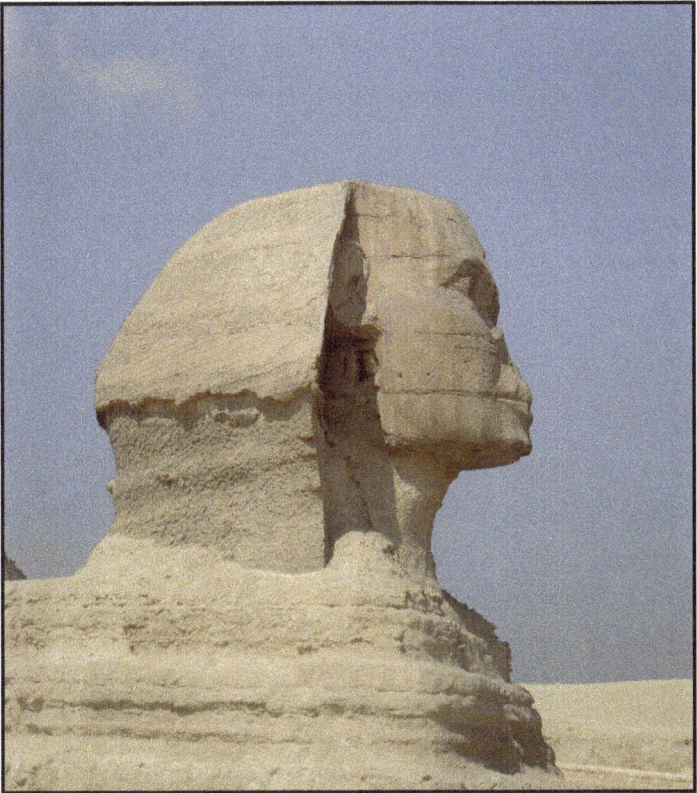

The Great Sphinx at Giza is an enormous stone statue with the body of a lion and a human's head. Some people believe it was built to guard the pyramids and crush the enemies who might try to rob the pharaoh's tombs.

The pharaoh, together with his treasures, was buried deep inside the pyramid in a special burial chamber. Sometimes fake burial chambers were built to fool grave robbers. Traps and curses were also put on the pyramids to try to protect their contents and keep the robbers out. Sadly most pyramids have been robbed of their contents.

Temples

Many temples were built by the pharaohs to honour their gods. The temple was made up of three parts - a small shrine, a large hall with many columns and an open courtyard. They would contain not only a place to worship but also beautiful gardens, large statues and memorials.

The temples were built of limestone with parts designed to look like plants. Some had columns to look like palm trees.

Temples were the heart of the community where children went to school and women brought offerings. It was a place to meet as well as to worship. Some famous temples are Luxor, the Temple of Amun at Karnak, the Temple of Isis at Philae, the Temple of Horus at Edfu and the Temples of Rameses and Nefertiti at Abu Simel.

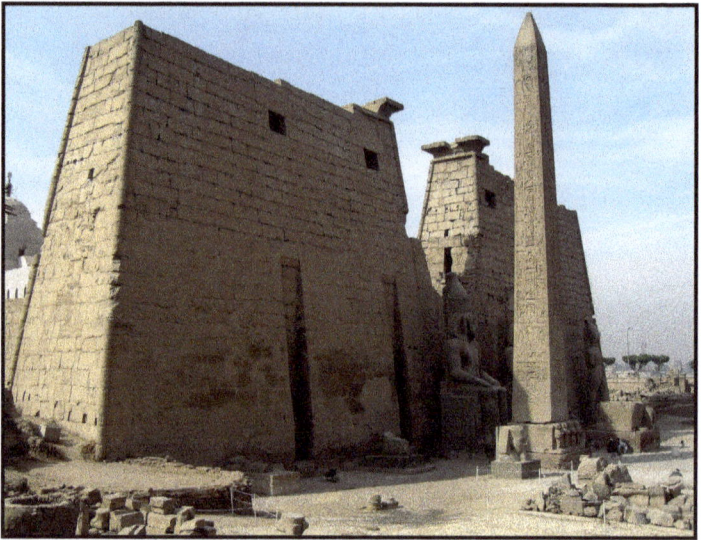

The Valley of the Kings

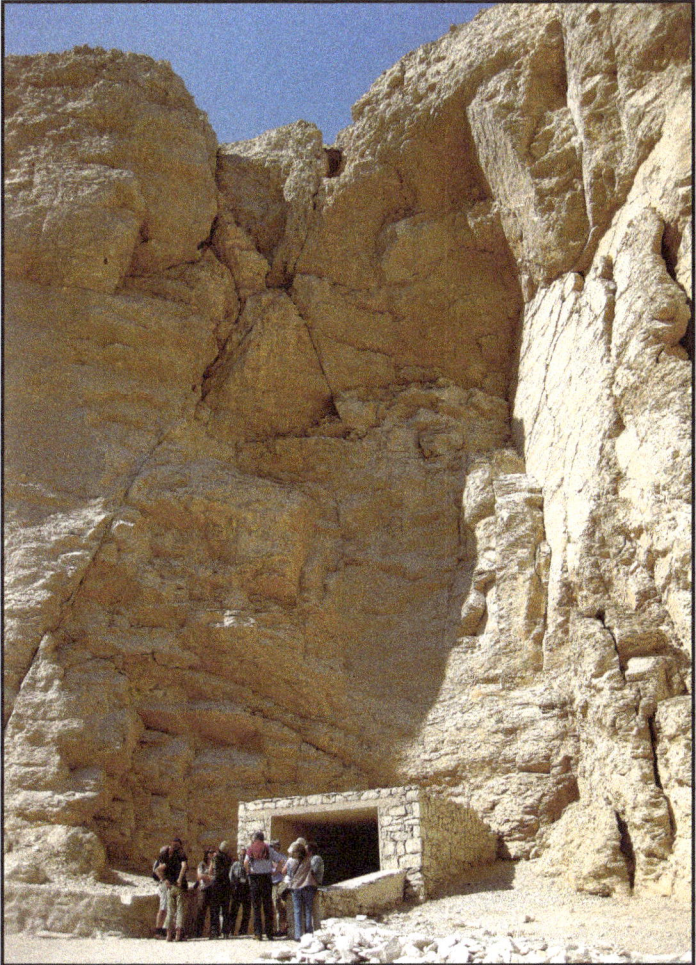

Around 1500 BC the pharaohs stopped building pyramids and choose instead to be buried in underground tombs in the Valley of the Kings. Here there are about 60 tombs of various sizes. Tuthmosis I was the first pharaoh to be buried in the Valley of the Kings.

Many tombs contained false entrances and burial chambers but again robbers still managed to plunder these tombs thousands of years ago, stealing the treasure. However, the artwork left on the walls has helped us to learn a lot about the lives of the Ancient Egyptians.

Amazingly one tomb held its secret for over 3000 years. It was the famous tomb of Tutankhamun which was discovered by Howard Carter in 1922.

Howard Carter discovers Tutankhamun

Howard Carter was an Englishman and archaeologist who had been working in Egypt for 31 years. He was convinced that there was one more tomb that had not been discovered. He had been searching for the tomb of Tutankhamun for five years, using the money of a wealthy Englishman called Lord Carnavon.

With so much money already spent Lord Carnavon almost gave up hope of finding the tomb but Howard Carter persuaded him to fund his work for one more year.

Carter had made a plan of the Valley of the Kings, convinced by the things already found that the tomb of Tutankhamun was definitely there. He re-examined these plans and noted that one place that had not been investigated was the pile of previously excavated earth, from other digs.

Searching through these mounds of earth Howard Carter's workmen found mud huts that had been left when building the tomb of Rameses VI.

Howard Carter and his men began to dig away the ground underneath them.

On the morning of 4th November 1922, a waterboy put down his water jars and hit his foot against a rock. The sand was scraped away to reveal that the rock was in fact a step. With excitement the workers cleared away more and more sand, revealing a whole flight of steps.

Howard Carter kept a diary and so we are able to read about the events that followed and share the excitement of the workers.

At the bottom of the steps they found a door, which had a stamp embedded within it. Without doubt Howard Carter knew that this was a sign that below the door someone of great importance was buried. Howard Carter was certain that it had never been disturbed but in spite of his excitement decided to wait for the arrival of Lord Carnavon before opening the door. They covered the door with sand to hide it.

A telegram was sent (no texts in those days) and it took three weeks before Lord Carnavon and his daughter arrived. With excitement the workmen again scraped away the sand and the door was completely revealed. Only now, on closer examination, did they discover that one of the seals had been broken and then resealed.

The door was removed and a passageway, filled with rubble, was revealed. Howard Carter was so disappointed because he realised that the tomb robbers had cut a way through the passageway. He now thought the burial chamber would now be empty.

While excavating the tomb a tablet was found with a curse written upon it. Howard Carter hid this tablet so that his workers would not know about it. He knew it was just something written to keep grave robbers away but did not want his men to be frightened.

With heavy hearts the workers cleared away the rubble from the passageway until they came to another door, which had also been disturbed. In his diary Howard Carter writes about how he made a tiny hole in the door 'with trembling hands'.

A candle was passed through the tiny hole and as their eyes gradually adjusted to the light they saw for the first time the wonderful treasures that the tomb still held. The hole was made bigger so that they could squeeze into the small room. Once in they found themselves surrounded with all the household treasures that Tutankhamun would need to travel safely through the Underworld to the Afterlife.

As they explored they found more and more rooms filled with amazing treasures fashioned from gold. Howard Carter believed he had discovered the most beautiful things ever to be found in Egypt. The tomb contained several chambers which included a burial chamber, antechamber, treasure chamber and annex.

Hieroglyphics

Much of what we know about the Ancient Egyptians comes from the hieroglyphic writing in their tombs and in their art. Hieroglyphics was a form of writing using pictures. Some pictures represented single letters while others whole words. The word Hieroglyphics come from two Greek words meaning 'Holy Writing'.

As well as writing on statues and tombs Egyptians also wrote on fine paper made from papyrus, a reed that grew by the Nile. They wrote using pens made from thin, sharp reeds using coloured inks or paints made from the plants that grew nearby.

The Rosetta Stone

Until the end of the 18th Century many things about the Ancient Egyptians had remained a mystery. No-one had been able to work out what the hieroglyphics represented or meant. We now know more about the Ancient Egyptians than any other civilisation due to the discovery of the Rosetta Stone.

In 1799 the Rosetta Stone was discovered by a group of French Soldiers who were rebuilding a fort near the Egyptian city of Rosetta. The Rosetta stone is just over a metre tall and dates from 196 BC when it had ancient laws inscribed upon it. Amazingly the laws were written in three scripts, two of which were Egyptian and the third Greek. It was written using hieroglyphics (used for important and religious documents), Demotic (used by the Egyptians for everyday writing) and Greek (used by the rulers of Egypt).

It took over twenty years to solve the mystery of the hieroglyphics on the stone. Jean Champollion, a French scholar, managed to work out what some pictures stood for and made sensible guesses about others using the Greek language to help him.

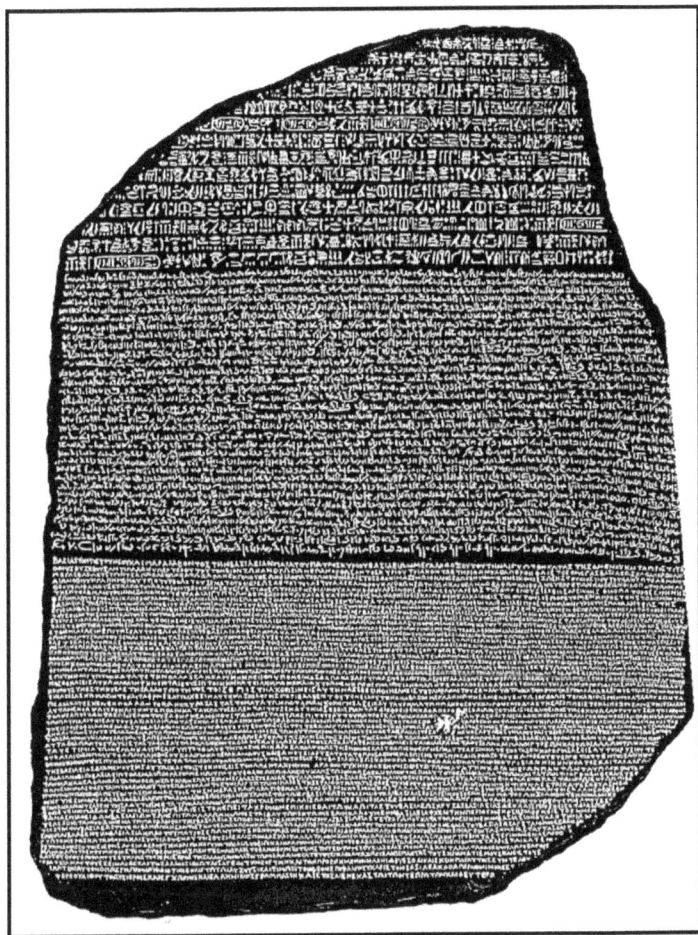

When the British defeated the French at the end of the Napoleonic Wars they claimed the Rosetta Stone and it was placed in the British Museum.

Gods and Goddesses

Gods and Goddesses played a big part in the lives of the Ancient Egyptians. There were many different ones and they could take on many different forms. Some took the form of animals while others had a human body with the head of an animal.

The same animal could represent a different god. It just depended upon where you lived or which temple you went for worship. There were over 2000 different gods but some were much more important than others.

Ra the God of the Sun was the most important god and known as lord of all the other gods. He was usually shown as a man with the head of falcon with the sun on top or a falcon crowned with a sun disk. The sun often has a cobra around it. The cobra also appears on the head of pharaohs such as Tutankhamun.

Ancient Egyptians believed that he created the world and that the rising sun was the symbol of creation. The legend says that each day Ra sails across the skies in a boat called 'Barque of Millions of Years'. He travels through twelve provinces, each representing an hour of daylight. His journey was not easy because on the way he had to fight his enemy, Apep the snake, but he did have other gods such as **Seth** and **Bastet** to help him.

At night he was thought to die, so left the moon to light the world, while he sailed through the Underworld, passing through twelve doors, each representing an hour of darkness. The next morning he was born again.

Anubis the God of Embalming was shown as having the head of a jackal or wild dog. He was the god of funerals and was often painted on the walls of the tombs to protect the dead from **Ammut**, the Devourer. Anubis was the guide of the dead as they made their way through the Underworld. He was thought to have invented embalming and used it on the first mummy **Osiris**. He was the keeper of poisons and medicines and was believed to have magical power.

Anubis was the one who performed the 'Weighing of the Heart Ceremony'. In the Hall of the Dead he weighed the heart against the feather of **Ma'at**, the goddess of justice, who sat on the top of the scales to ensure the weighing was carried out properly.

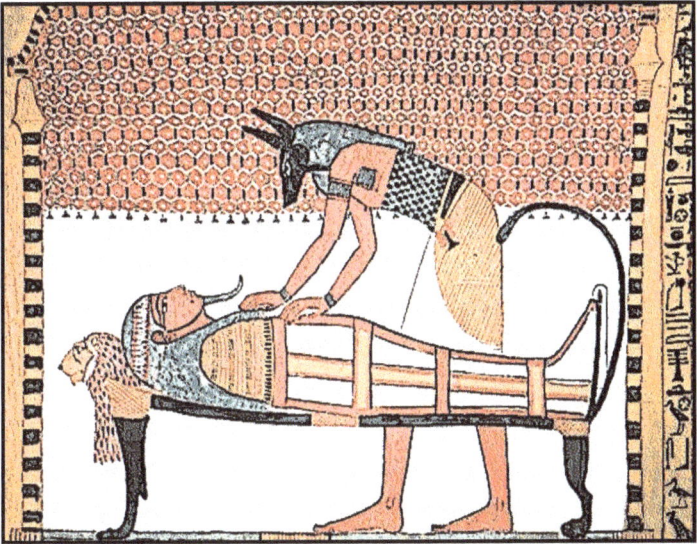

If the heart was heavier than the feather then **Ammut,** who had the head of a crocodile, the shoulders of a lion and the backside of a hippopotamus, would eat you. Today we still use the expressions 'a heart as light as a feather' when we feel cheerful and 'heavy-hearted' when we are unhappy.

Osiris the god of the dead was ruler of the Underworld. All pharaohs became an Osiris when they died. Osiris is shown as a man with a beard wearing bandages like a mummy. He wore a white crown surrounded by red feathers.

Osiris was the husband of **Isis** and the father of **Horus**. He was killed by his brother of **Seth** who wanted to take his place as pharaoh. Luckily his wife found him and bought him back to life.

Isis the goddess of love and motherhood and is shown with a throne or sun disk with horns on her head. She was the mother of Horus and the wife and sister of Osiris.

Isis was also a great healer and magician, getting her magic power by tricking Ra, the sun god. She taught mankind to use medicines. Isis is often found at the foot of coffins, protecting the body with her long wings.

Horus god of the sky is shown as a falcon or a man having the head of a falcon. Horus lost his eye after fighting Seth, who killed his father. The eye of Horus was healed by Thoth and was used as an amulet (magic charm).

It was believed that Horus gave power to each pharaoh and that the pharaoh was the 'Living Horus'.

Bastet goddess of cats, women and children is shown as a woman with a cat's head or as a cat.

The Ancient Egyptians believed that cats were sacred. They killed the rats and mice that ate the grain and caused disease. If you killed a cat in these times then you would be punished by death. Bastet helped defend Ra against the snake Apep when he tried to stop her father's journey through the Underworld at night.

Hapi was god of the Nile and for those living near to the Nile even more important than Ra, the sun god. Although the Egyptians knew that without the sun they would live in darkness they knew that without the waters of the Nile they would die.

He is shown as a bearded man, often coloured blue - probably to represent the water of the Nile. It was believed that the source of the Niles waters came from two whirlpools and that Hapi's journey took him through the Underworld and the Heavens before arriving in Egypt.

Thoth the god of knowledge was responsible for giving the Egyptians writing, mathematics and medicine. He was also god of the moon. He is shown as a man with the head of an ibis and also as a baboon.

Thoth helped Isis bring Osiris back from the dead. He was the measurer of the earth, counter of the stars and the keeper and recorder of all knowledge. He was also the god who recorded the results at the 'Weighing of the Heart Ceremony'.

Conclusion

Throughout this book you will have learnt how extraordinary and amazing the Ancient Egyptians were. They taught the rest of the world so many things. The Ancient Egyptians created the world's first form of government and developed one of the first religions to value life after death.

They invented a form of paper, a kind of picture writing, forms of arithmetic and even a 365 day calendar.

The people were knowledgeable, practical and creative with brilliant architects, builders, sculptures, painters, doctors and a wealth of other craftsmen.

The pyramids and temples that still stand should always remind us of the marvellous civilization of Ancient Egypt and all it contributed to our knowledge today.

The Quiz

Questions

Daily Life (1)

1. What was the main food of the poor?

2. How was food baked?

3. What was the most popular drink?

4. What grain was used to make it?

5. What material was used to make clothes?

6. Why was this material chosen?

7. What did Egyptians use to build their houses?

8. Where did they get their materials?

9. Why did their houses have flat roofs?

10. Why were the windows narrow and high up?

Daily Life (2)

11. Who wore jewellery and make up in Ancient Egyptian times?

12. What material was used by the poor people to make their jewellery?

13. What was the most common job?

14. What did people who could read and write do?

15. Did Egyptians keep cats as pets?

16. What did people sometimes do when their cat died?

17. What materials were used to make toys?

18. Why did poor children have toys made of clay?

19. Did children play with plastic footballs?

20. Did Egyptians use money to buy things they needed?

Pyramids, Tombs and Temples (1)

21.   Why were pyramids built?

22.   What is the shape of each base?

23.   What is the earliest known pyramid?

24.   Why is it thought the earlier pyramids were built with steps?

25.   Which is the largest pyramid?

26.   How many blocks were needed to build it?

27.   Why is the pyramid build for Pharaoh Sneferu bent?

28.   Where can you find most Egyptian pyramids?

29.   Why have many original treasures disappeared from the pyramids?

30.   Why were traps and false passages put in pyramids?

Pyramids, Tombs and Temples (2)

31. What was the Rosetta Stone and why was it so important?

32. How tall is the Giant Pyramid at Giza?

33. What is the Valley of the Kings?

34. Whose tomb was found with almost all the contents untouched?

35. Who discovered this tomb?

36. Why did many tombs have false entrances?

37. Why had Tutankhamun's tomb not been discovered before and raided?

38. How many tombs are there in the Valley of the Kings?

39. Who was the first pharaoh to be buried here?

40. Why are so many ruins of pyramids still standing?

The River Nile (1)

41. How long is the River Nile?

42. Into which sea does the River Nile flow?

43. How often did the River Nile flood?

44. What caused the Nile to flood?

45. Why was flooding a good thing for the Ancient Egyptians?

46. Why does the River Nile no longer flood today?

47. How did the Ancient Egyptians get the water from the Nile up to their fields?

48. What was the clay from the Nile used for?

49. Why was Egypt known as 'The Gift of the Nile'?

50. What did the Egyptians call the land next to the Nile?

The River Nile (2)

51. What was the Red Land?

52. Although nothing could grow there why was it useful for Egypt to have large deserts?

53. What would happen in the years when the Nile hardly flooded at all?

54. Why did they build reservoirs to hold the flood water?

55. Besides crops what else did the Nile provide for people to eat?

56. What else did the Egyptians make from papyrus besides paper?

57. What was the quickest way to travel and transport goods in Ancient Egypt?

58. In which direction did the River Nile flow?

59. What was special about the west bank of the Nile?

60. Who was god of the Nile?

Farming

61. How many seasons did the farmers recognise in Ancient Egypt?

62. What were they called?

63. When did the Ancient Egyptians plant the grain?

64. What animals were used to tramp the seed into the ground?

65. What did the farmers do when the land was flooded?

66. Besides food crops what other plant grew along the Nile?

67. For what did the Egyptians use it?

68. What materials were used for tools?

69. What did the farmers plant after they had harvested the grain crops like wheat and barley?

70. Why did they plant vines and fruit trees along the paths?

The Pharaohs (1)

71. What job did the pharaoh do?

72. What did the Ancient Egyptians believe pharaohs were?

73. What does the word pharaoh mean?

74. What was the time for which a family of pharaohs ruled known as?

75. Which pharaoh banished all gods except Ra, the sun god?

76. Who was the last pharaoh of the Ancient Egyptians?

77. Which civilization conquered the Ancient Egyptians?

78. Which pharaoh had more monuments built to himself than any other?

79. What did pharaohs use to protect themselves?

80. How old was Tutankhamun when he became pharaoh?

The Pharaohs (2)

81. Which pharaoh built the first pyramid?

82. What did the pharaohs build to honour their gods?

83. Where were the first pharaohs buried?

84. Why did the Egyptians put curses on the pyramids?

85. Who was the first pharaoh who united the north and south Kingdoms of Egypt?

86. Who was the longest ruling pharaoh?

87. How long did he reign?

88. Which pharaoh is remembered for her great beauty?

89. Which pharaoh ruled for her son and dressed as a male pharaoh?

90. How did Cleopatra die?

Mummification (1)

91. What is an Egyptian mummy?

92. Why did the Ancient Egyptians embalm the bodies of their pharaohs?

93. What is Natron and why was it used?

94. How long was the body left to dry out?

95. What was used to stuff the bodies?

96. How did the Ancient Egyptians get the brain out of a body?

97. Why did they throw it away?

98. What happened to the important organs in the body?

99. Why was the heart left inside the body?

100. What is a shroud?

Mummification (2)

101. What is a sarcophagus?

102. Why was it important to preserve the body after death?

103. What was the Afterlife?

104. What was done to the body before embalming began?

105. What was special about the tops of canopic jars?

106. What was the 'Weighing of the Heart Ceremony'?

107. What was rubbed onto the body to stop it from wrinkling?

108. What is an amulet?

109. How did the dead person's spirit recognise the body in the Afterlife?

110. Why was the pharaoh buried with all his possessions?

Gods and Goddesses (1)

111. What form did gods and goddesses take?

112. Who was the most important god?

113. What was Osiris god of?

114. Of which god was pharaoh the living version?

115. Who looked after the world when Ra died at night?

116. How many doors did Ra have to pass through when travelling through the Underworld at night?

117. Thoth was god of two things. What were they?

118. Who is found at the foot of coffins, protecting the body with her long wings?

119. Who was the god of embalming?

120. What was the name of the snake that Ra had to fight?

Gods and Goddesses (2)

121. Which god did the Ancient Egyptians believe to have created the world?

122. Who was the god who guided the dead as they made their way through the Underworld.

123. What did he look like?

124. What was used to weigh the heart against in the ceremony performed by Anubis?

125. What god were all pharaohs thought to become when they died?

126. Who was the god known as the Devourer?

127. What did he look like?

128. Who was the god of the dead and ruler of the Underworld?

129. Who killed Osiris and why?

130. Which goddess got her magic power by tricking the sun god Ra and taught the world to use medicines?

General Questions (1)

131. Who was the supreme ruler of Ancient Egypt?

132. Why was this so?

133. Who was second in charge, after the pharaoh?

134. How many dynasties were there in Ancient Egypt?

135. From what was paper made?

136. Was what Ancient Egyptian picture writing called?

137. What was used to sweeten food?

138. What did a scribe do?

139. When did Howard Carter discover Tutankhamun's tomb?

140. Who provided the money for Howard Carter to search for so many years for this tomb?

General Questions (2)

141. In the pyramid of importance who were at the bottom of the pyramid?

142. Name four skilled craftsmen who worked in Ancient Egypt.

143. Who conquered Egypt bringing to an end the last dynasty of pharaohs for the Ancient Egyptians?

144. What was found in tombs that allowed us to find out so much about Ancient Egypt?

145. How did Ancient Egyptians preserve their food?

146. Why did Howard Carter hide the tablet with the curse written upon it from his workers?

147. How do we know in such detail what happened when Tutankhamun's tomb was discovered?

148. Why was Howard Carter so disappointed when he finally reached the first door of the tomb and examined it?

149. Was it easy to reach the second door by travelling along the passageway from the first door?

150. How many years did it take to solve the mystery of the Rosetta stone?

Answers

Daily Life (1)

1. Bread and vegetables.

2. In a clay oven.

3. Beer.

4. Barley.

5. Linen.

6. Egypt is a very hot country and this material helped to keep you cool.

7. Mud bricks that had been baked in the sun.

8. Clay from the River Nile and straw from the fields.

9. So they could sleep safely outside when it was hot.

10. To stop so much sun entering their houses and heating the inside in summer.

Daily Life (2)

11. Both men and women.

12. Copper.

13. Farming.

14. They became scribes and kept records for the pharaoh.

15. No. Most houses had one but they were sacred animals.

16. They shaved their eyebrows.

17. Ivory, marble, ceramics, clay and stone.

18. It was cheap and readily available.

19. No. They used leather skins stuffed with straw or reeds and tied with string.

20. No. They used a barter system in which they exchanged one type of goods for another.

Pyramids, Tombs and Temples (1)

21. They were built as tombs and monuments for the pharaohs.

22. Square.

23. The stepped pyramid of Djoser [Zozer] at Saqqara.

24. It is thought they were stairways so the pharaoh could climb them to reach the sun god.

25. The Giant Pyramid at Giza, built for the pharaoh Khufu.

26. Two million.

27. Because they started building it using the wrong angle. They had to change the slope of the sides as it would have been too tall, too expensive to build, and unsafe.

28. Most were built on the western side of the Nile.

29. Because over the years they have been stolen by tomb robbers.

30. To trick the robbers into thinking there was no treasure.

Pyramids, Tombs and Temples (2)

31. It was a large piece of stone on which laws had been written in 196BC. These laws were written in three scripts and helped people work out what the hieroglyphics found in Egypt actually meant.

32. It is 139 metres tall.

33. A valley where pharaohs' tombs are hidden underground rather than in pyramids.

34. Tutankhamun.

35. Howard Carter.

36. To fool tomb robbers so they did not find the treasure.

37. The steps leading to the entrance were hidden underneath workmen's huts.

38. About 60.

39. Tuthmosis I

40. Because they have been well preserved due to Egypt's hot and dry climate.

The River Nile (1)

41.   6650 kilometres (4132 miles).

42.   The Mediterranean.

43.   Every year.

44.   The melting mountain snows and heavy summer rainfall.

45.   When the river overflowed its banks a layer of rich silt was left behind, making the ground very fertile.

46.   A large dam has been built at Aswan which controls the flow of the water.

47.   They used a shaduf, or a series of shadufs.

48.   Making clay bricks for housing and also building reservoirs to hold the water after the flood.

49.   The Nile provided all the things that the Egyptians needed.

50.   Kemet - The Black Land

The River Nile (2)

51. The desert, know to the Egyptians as Deshret.

52. It protected Egypt from invasion.

53. There would be a poor harvest and a danger that people would starve.

54. Egypt was so hot and dry in the summer that the crops would die without extra irrigation.

55. Fish from its waters and birds that lived along its banks.

56. Boats.

57. Along the River Nile.

58. Northwards.

59. This was where most Pharaohs were buried.

60. Hapi.

Farming

61. Three.

62. Akhet, the flooding season; Peret, the growing season; Shemu, the harvesting season.

63. Once the floods had gone down.

64. Cattle.

65. They mended their tools, looked after their animals and worked for the pharaoh building pyramids.

66. Papyrus.

67. Paper and making boats.

68. Wood, stone and copper.

69. Vegetables.

70. To shade other plants from the harsh summer sun.

The Pharaohs (1)

71. The pharaoh was the head of the government and the most important High Priest.

72. Half man, half god.

73. Great House.

74. A dynasty.

75. Nefertiti and her husband Akhenaten.

76. Cleopatra.

77. The Romans.

78. Ramesses II.

79. They wore a crown decorated with a cobra, representing the Cobra goddess.

80. He was only 9.

The Pharaohs (2)

81. Netjerykhet

82. Temples and monuments.

83. In the sand on the western bank of the Nile.

84. To frighten the grave robbers and stop them from stealing the treasure in tombs and pyramids.

85. Menes.

86. Ramasses II

87. He reigned for 67 years.

88. Nefertiti.

89. Hatsheput.

90. She killed herself with a poisonous snake called an asp.

Mummification (1)

91. A body that has been embalmed so it is preserved.

92. To preserve a body for as long as possible so that it could make the journey to the Afterlife.

93. A kind of salt that was used to dry out the body.

94. It took about 40 days.

95. Sawdust, spices, leaves and linen.

96. They used a hook to pull it out through the nose.

97. They thought it was worthless.

98. They were put into canopic jars.

99. They believed it was the centre of intelligence and would be needed in the afterlife.

100. A cloth that is used to wrap the mummy after it has been embalmed.

Mummification (2)

101. A special box, shaped like a body, in which the mummy was put.

102. So that it was preserved to travel safely through the Underworld into the Afterlife.

103. A perfect version of Ancient Egypt.

104. It was purified by washing it in the River Nile.

105. They were shaped to look like heads of animals or humans.

106. The heart was weighed against a feather to see if the person had led a good or bad life.

107. Special oil.

108. A good luck charm.

109. Their face was painted upon the sarcophagus.

110. So that he would have everything he needed in the Afterlife.

Gods and Goddesses (1)

111. Some took the form of animals while others had a human body with the head of an animal.

112. Ra, the sun god.

113. God of the dead.

114. Horus.

115. The moon god.

116. Twelve to represent the twelve hours of nightime.

117. He was god of all knowledge as well as god of the moon.

118. Isis.

119. Anubis.

120. Apep.

Gods and Goddesses (2)

121. Ra, the sun god.

122. Anubis.

123. He had the head of a jackal or wild dog.

124. The feather of Ma'at.

125. Osiris.

126. Ammut.

127. He had the head of a crocodile, the shoulders of a lion and the backside of a hippopotamus.

128. Osiris.

129. His brother Seth who wanted to take his place as pharaoh.

130. Isis.

General Questions (1)

131. The pharaoh.

132. He was head of the government, the most important High priest and people thought him to be half man and half god.

133. The Vizier.

134. There were 31.

135. Papyrus.

136. Hieroglyphics.

137. Honey.

138. He kept records about life in Egypt such as how much food was harvested and how many soldiers were in the army.

139. On the 4th November 1922.

140. Lord Carnavon.

General Questions (2)

141. Slaves, labourers and peasants

142. Jewellery makers, weavers, painters, tailors, carpenters and potters.

143. The Romans.

144. Pictures on the walls and objects that Egyptians used in everyday life.

145. By drying it.

146. He knew they were frightened of the curses that were put on tombs and would no longer work for him.

147. Howard Carter kept a detailed diary of everything that happened.

148. He noticed that the seals had been broken and thought that tomb robbers had stolen the treasure.

149. No, it was full of rubble and rocks.

150. Twenty years.

www.ingramcontent.com/pod-product-compliance
Lightning Source LLC
LaVergne TN
LVHW010315070426
835510LV00024B/3394

9781782345640